House of Commons

Registration of Assurances (Ireland) Bill

House of Commons

Registration of Assurances (Ireland) Bill

ISBN/EAN: 9783741199875

Manufactured in Europe, USA, Canada, Australia, Japa

Cover: Foto ©Lupo / pixelio.de

Manufactured and distributed by brebook publishing software
(www.brebook.com)

House of Commons

Registration of Assurances (Ireland) Bill

This Bill, and the Local Registration of Title (Ireland) Bill, are intended to place the entire system of land registry in Ireland on a satisfactory basis, with special reference to recent legislation, and to the recent multiplication of the number of small proprietors.

There has been established in Ireland since 1708 a general Registry of Deeds, in its main features similar to the systems which exist in Scotland, Yorkshire, and Middlesex. It is not proposed to abolish this system, which is generally accepted as satisfactory, but to develop, simplify, and improve it, in accordance with recommendations made by Royal Commissions, and Parliamentary and Treasury Committees on different occasions during the past half century.

Leaving to the Local Registration of Title Bill the work of providing for the smaller proprietors in Ireland a system of local registration of title, the present Bill deals with the existing general Registry of Deeds, in regard to which its main objects are:—

1. To consolidate the numerous statutes relating to the registration of deeds, judgments, and judgment-mortgages in Ireland, which have been passed from the reign of Queen Anne to the present time.

2. To simplify and cheapen the practice as regards registration by dispensing with certain useless and expensive processes which have been retained from the earlier statutes, and by adopting the ordnance survey as the basis of registration.

3. To afford complete safety to purchasers, by bringing within the range of the registry certain classes of dealings with land, against which no protection is now afforded; by excluding the equitable doctrines of notice as regards registered instruments; and by affording protection to contracts by means of caveats.

4. To consolidate with the registry of deeds the existing registry of judgments; providing for the re-registration in the registry of deeds of the class of judgments which now operate by way of general charge on the land of the judgment debtor; such re-registration to be effected as against specified lands.

5. To afford protection to the public and to solicitors against the consequences of possible technical errors, by providing that the certificate of the registrar shall be conclusive evidence of registration. The cases in which registration has been held invalid are generally cases of extreme hardship, and the error has seldom been of a kind likely to mislead.

A.D. 1891.

6. To provide for the regulation of office details by general rules. For this purpose it is proposed to place the office under the management of the Land Judge.

Many clauses of this Bill are borrowed from an Act, the commencement of which was deferred until the issuing of a Treasury Minute (13 & 14 Vict. c. 72). This statute contained many valuable provisions, mainly founded on the second report of the Real Property Commission, 1832; but the system of indexes which it introduced was found to be unworkable, and it was never brought into operation. From it are taken (with certain modifications) the clauses as to the registration of orders affecting land and private Acts of Parliament (cl. 8), of equitable mortgages and vendors' lien (cl. 10–12), of wills and intestacies (cl. 13–20), the adoption of the ordnance maps as the basis of registration (cl. 37), the provisions as to notice (cl. 59), and caveats (cl. 62–64).

These enactments and most of the other provisions of this Bill (with the exceptions herein-after mentioned) are in general accordance with the recommendations of a Royal Commission appointed in 1878, to inquire into the registration of deeds and judgments, which had among its legal members the Lord Chief Justice (Mr. May), the Lord Chief Baron, the Vice-Chancellor, the Right Honourable Mountifort Longfield, and other lawyers of eminence. The first report of this Commission was presented in 1879, and the second in the following year. The main points on which this Bill departs from the report of the Commission are: (1.) In retaining the system of registration by memorial, which has been in use since the establishment of the office (while simplifying the memorial, and dispensing with certain useless formalities), instead of the system recommended by the Commission, of depositing a copy of the instrument registered, with an abstract for the purpose of registration. The memorial will be so framed as to form the foundation of the indexes and books kept in the office, but the responsibility for its accuracy in such matters as the distinction between grantors and grantees for purposes of registration, will rest with the office, on which is cast the duty of comparison, and (if necessary) of amendment. (2.) In providing for the deposit of certified copies of assurances, at the option of the persons tendering them for registration. Memorials are often so framed as to afford some kind of secondary evidence of the contents of deeds. However unsatisfactory they may be in this point of view it does not appear desirable to interfere with the usefulness of the memorial in this particular without providing a more efficient substitute for those who desire to use the registry, not merely for the purpose of giving

notice of registered assurances, but as preserving evidence of their
contents. (3.) In retaining the existing system of judgment
mortgages, instead of providing for the immediate realization of
judgments by sale of the debtor's land; a proposal which was
recommended by the Commission, but which is unsuitable to
the existing condition of the country. (4.) In adopting a still
further simplification of proof for purposes of registration. (5.)
In some matters relating to the registration of wills. The Irish
Registry Acts, though providing for the registration of wills,
contain no provisions for the protection of purchasers from
persons claiming under unregistered wills, differing in this respect
from the Yorkshire and Middlesex Acts. The Irish Act of 1850
(13 & 14 Vict. c. 72.) contained provisions for this purpose,
which have been in substance adopted in the present Bill. These
provisions differ in some particulars from the recommendations
contained in the Report of the Royal Commission of 1878, which,
however, adopts the general principle of protecting purchasers
from claims under unregistered wills. (6.) In adopting from
13 & 14 Vict. c. 72. the system of registration of intestacies, with
additional provisions for the protection of persons claiming under
wills which may have been mislaid or suppressed. This system,
since the Report of 1878, was introduced in the year 1884 into
the Act consolidating and amending the law relating to the Yorkshire registry of deeds, and received the sanction of the Legislature
as regards Ireland in 1850.

Registration of Assurances (Ireland) Bill.

ARRANGEMENT OF CLAUSES.

PART II.

WILLS AND INTESTACIES.

Clause.

13. Registration of wills.
14. Affidavit of intestacy may be registered after six months.
15. Unregistered will void against purchasers under registered will or under a registered intestacy.

Provision for Cases of disputed Intestacy.

16. When will cannot be registered within two years, persons claiming under it may obtain an order to register intestacy as disputed.
17. Affidavit of intestacy may be registered while intestacy registered as disputed.
18. Provision for cases of disputed intestacy.
19. Removal of note of intestacy as disputed, and cancelling of registration of affidavit of intestacy.
20. Cancelling registration of will probate of which has been revoked.

PART III.

JUDGMENTS AND JUDGMENT MORTGAGES.

Judgments, Lis pendens, Crown Bonds, Recognizances, &c.

21. Judgments, &c. entered up before 15th July 1850, recognizances, Crown bonds, and lis pendens invalid as against purchasers, &c., unless registered within five years.
22. Abolition of Registry of Judgments and index of judgments to be kept.
23. Provision for registration of judgments, &c. in the Registry Office.
24. No judgments, lis pendens, recognizance, &c. to affect land other than that specified in the memorial.
25. Registrar to give certificate of registry.
26. Memorandum of satisfaction of judgments, &c. may be lodged in Registry Office.

Judgment Mortgages.

PART IV.

How Registration shall be effected.

Ordnance Map to be the basis of Registry.

Registration to be by Memorial.

Provisional Registration in certain Cases.

PART V.

GENERAL PROVISIONS.

Certificate of Registration.

PART VI.

SEARCHES.

PART VII.

CONSTITUTION OF THE OFFICE.—STAMPS AND FEES.

Stamps and Fees.

PART VIII.

GENERAL RULES, AND MISCELLANEOUS PROVISIONS.

Extension of Time.

Affidavits.

A

· BILL

TO

Consolidate and amend the Laws relating to the Regis-   A.D. 1891.
tration of Deeds and Judgments, and to provide for
the Registration of other assurances, acts, and matters
affecting Land in Ireland.

BE it enacted by the Queen's most Excellent Majesty, by and
with the advice and consent of the Lords Spiritual and Tem-
poral, and Commons, in this present Parliament assembled, and by
the authority of the same, as follows :

5   *Preliminary.*

1. This Act may be cited as the Registration of Assurances   Short title.
(Ireland) Act, 1891.

2. This Act shall extend to Ireland only.   Act to extend to Ireland only.

3. This Act shall, except as in this Act specially provided, come   Commencement of the Act.
10 into operation on the *first day of January one thousand eight
hundred and ninety-two.*

PART I.

ASSURANCES.

General Provisions.

15   4. Any assurance made or executed after the *twenty-fifth day of*   Assurances executed after the 25th of
March one thousand seven hundred and eight in any way affecting   March 1708 may be registered.
land may, subject to the provisions of this Act, be registered at the   [6 Anne, c. 2.]
election of any person concerned.

20   5. Every such assurance which shall be registered shall be good   Every registered assurance effectual accord-
and effectual, both in law and equity, according to the priority of   ing to priority of
time of registering the same, for and concerning the land men-   registering, against all
tioned in the memorial for the registration thereof, according to   other assur-
the right, title, and interest of the person conveying or assuring
[Bill 190.]   A

A.D. 1891.

such land, against every other assurance or disposition of the same land, or of any part thereof.

6. Every assurance or disposition made or executed after the twenty-fifth day of March one thousand seven hundred and eight and not registered, affecting all or any of the lands mentioned in 5 the memorial of a registered assurance, shall be fraudulent and void, not only against such registered assurance, but likewise against all creditors by judgment or recognizance, confessed, acknowledged, or entered into after the twenty-fifth day of March aforesaid, as for and concerning all or any of the land mentioned in the memorial 10 of the registered Assurance.

7. Nothing in this Act shall require the registration of any lease for years not exceeding *thirty-one years*, or any assurance affecting any land demised by the lease, where actual possession goes along with the lease or assurance, or of any will or affidavit of intestacy 15 affecting the same.

Private Acts and Orders affecting Land.

8. Any private Act of Parliament or order affecting land passed or made after the commencement of this Act may be registered by any person claiming any interest thereunder; but nothing in this 20 Act contained shall require the registration of any private Act of Parliament or order affecting land passed or made before the commencement thereof.

Vesting of Lands under Act of Parliament; Equitable Mortgage; and Vendor's lien for Purchase Money.   25

9. Where the provisions of any Act of Parliament passed or to be passed have the effect of vesting land in any person by or upon the payment of money, or by or upon any other act (other than any assurance or disposition authorised to be registered), and the land becomes so vested by or upon any such payment or other 30 act, made or done after the commencement of this Act, any person claiming under or by virtue of such vesting may register a memorandum in the prescribed form, containing a reference to the Act of Parliament, and stating the denominations on the ordnance map, and the payment or other act by or upon which the land has 35 so vested; and such memorandum shall be deemed to be an assurance for the purposes of this Act; but nothing in this section contained shall apply to the vesting of the estate of a bankrupt in the assignees or trustee of such bankrupt.

10. Any person claiming an interest under an equitable mortgage made after the commencement of this Act may register a memorandum, in the prescribed form, stating the principal sum of money secured by such equitable mortgage; or in case the total amount 5 of the principal money secured thereby is limited not to exceed a given sum, the total amount of such principal sum; or in case the money secured thereby is without any limit, that the money so secured is unlimited; and stating the denominations on the ordnance map, and such memorandum shall be deemed to be an assurance 10 for the purposes of this Act.

11. Where, by reason of the nonpayment of purchase money, a vendor, after the commencement of this Act, acquires a lien for any purchase money, any person claiming an interest in the lien may register a memorandum in the prescribed form, con-15 taining such particulars of the conveyance by the vendor as are prescribed; stating the amount of the money for which a lien is claimed; and also stating the denominations on the ordnance map, and such memorandum shall be deemed to be an assurance for the purposes of this Act.

20 12.—(1.) In the several cases of a private Act of Parliament, order affecting land, vesting under Act of Parliament, equitable mortgage, and vendor's lien, the assurance to be registered shall for the purposes of this Act be deemed to have been made by the person whose estate or interest in the lands is affected by the private Act, 25 order, vesting, equitable mortgage, or lien (as the case may be), and such person shall for the purposes of this Act be deemed to be the grantor in respect of each such assurance. Every person claiming or deriving any right or title under any vesting under Act of Parliament, equitable mortgage, or vendor's lien, as the case 30 may be, in respect of which a memorandum is registered under the provisions of this Act, shall for the purposes of this Act be deemed to claim or derive such right or title under the memorandum so registered as an assurance.

PART II.

35 ### WILLS AND INTESTACIES.

13. Any will affecting land, when the testator dies after the commencement of this Act, may be registered by any devisee thereunder, in the manner hereinafter provided.

[190.] A 2

A.D. 1891.

Affidavit of intestacy may be registered after six months.
[14 & 15 Vict. c. 72, s. 13.]

14.—(1.) Any person claiming any estate or interest in land, as heir or otherwise, which might have been defeated or affected by the will of any person dying after the commencement of this Act, and who believes such person to have died intestate, or intestate as to such land, may at any time after (but not before) the expiration of six months from the death of such person make an affidavit in the prescribed form, and such affidavit (in this Act referred to as an "affidavit of intestacy") may be registered in the registry office in the prescribed manner   5

(2.) Every such affidavit shall state—   10
(a.) The date of the death of the deceased.
(b.) The name and addition of the deceased.
(c.) The name and addition of the deponent.
(d.) The denominations on the ordnance map of the land intended to be affected by the registration.   15
(e.) The nature of the estate or interest claimed by the deponent.
(f.) The fact that the deponent believes that the deceased died intestate, or intestate as to the land.

Unregistered will and assurances under registered will registered as against registered assurance.
[14 & 15 Vict. c. 11, s. 27.]

15.—(1.) When any will authorised to be registered under this Act is registered, every other will executed by the same testator   20 shall, as regards the land against which such first-mentioned will is registered, be void, as against any person claiming for valuable consideration under any registered assurance executed by any devisee under such first-mentioned will, unless such other will has been registered before the registration of such assurance.   25

(2.) When an affidavit of intestacy is registered, any will executed by the person in respect of whose intestacy such affidavit is so registered shall, as regards the land against which such affidavit of intestacy is registered, be void, as against any person claiming for valuable consideration under any registered assurance executed by   30 any person claiming immediately or derivatively under such intestacy, unless such will has been registered before the registration of such assurance.

(3.) Every will registered within *two years* after the death of the testator, or while his intestacy shall continue to be registered   35 as disputed under the provisions of this Act, shall be as valid and effectual as if it had been registered immediately after his death, and the date of the registration of every will registered

within such period shall for the purposes of this Act be deemed
to be the date of the death of the testator.

Provision for Cases of disputed Intestacy.

16.—(1.) When any person claiming to be interested under the
5 alleged will of a person dying after the commencement of this
Act is unable to register such will within the period of two years
from the death of such person, by reason of the concealment,
suppression, or contesting of such will, or any other cause, such
person may apply to the High Court within the said period, in
10 the prescribed manner, for liberty to register as disputed the
intestacy of the person under whose alleged will he claims; and
the High Court, if satisfied that there is reasonable ground for
disputing such intestacy, may direct that a memorial of the disputed intestacy shall be received and registered, and may by order
15 limit or extend the time during which the intestacy shall continue
registered as disputed.

(2.) The registrar, upon production to him of such order, and of
a memorial in the prescribed form, stating the name and addition
of the person so dying, the date of his death, and the denominations
20 on the ordnance map, shall register the intestacy of such person
as disputed; and upon the determination of the time limited by
such order as aforesaid the registration of the intestacy as disputed
shall be cancelled and avoided.

17. Nothing herein contained shall prevent the registration of
25 an affidavit of intestacy while the intestacy shall continue registered as disputed, but in such case the registration of every such
affidavit of intestacy shall be noted as disputed in the prescribed
manner; and if the will of the person whose intestacy has been
registered as disputed shall be registered within the aforesaid
30 period of two years, then the registration of the affidavit of
intestacy shall be cancelled, and shall have thenceforth no operation
or effect whatever; otherwise such registration shall be effectual
as from the date at which it shall have been effected.

18.—(1.) When an affidavit of intestacy has been registered,
35 and proceedings are taken, at any time after such registration,
in a court of competent jurisdiction for the purpose of obtaining
probate of the will of the person in respect of whose intestacy

the affidavit is registered, or for the purpose of obtaining letters of administration with the will annexed, it shall be lawful for any person claiming under the will to require the registrar to note the fact that the intestacy is disputed, and the registrar, upon proof in the prescribed manner of the institution of such proceedings, shall note the intestacy as disputed in the prescribed manner, and thenceforth, and so long as the intestacy shall be noted as disputed, the registration of the affidavit of intestacy shall have no operation or effect whatever.

(2.) Nothing in this section contained shall affect in any way the 10 priority herein-before given to any person claiming for valuable consideration under any registered assurance executed by any person claiming immediately or derivatively under an intestacy an affidavit of which has been registered under this Act, where the assurance has been registered prior to the noting of the intestacy 15 as disputed.

10.—(1.) When the registration of any affidavit of intestacy is noted as disputed, if the proceedings for the purpose of obtaining probate of the will of the person in respect of whose intestacy the affidavit is so registered as aforesaid, or of obtaining letters of 20 administration with his will annexed, terminate in the refusal of the court to grant probate of the will or such letters of administration, any person claiming under the intestacy may apply to the registrar to cancel the noting of the intestacy as disputed; and the registrar, upon proof to him in the prescribed manner 25 of the termination of such proceedings in the manner aforesaid, shall cancel the noting of the intestacy as disputed, and upon such note being so cancelled the registration of the affidavit of intestacy shall have the same effect and operation as from the date of its registration as if the intestacy had not been noted as 30 disputed.

(2.) In the event of the proceedings for obtaining such probate or letters of administration terminating in the granting of such probate or letters of administration, the registrar shall, upon proof to him in the prescribed manner of the granting of such 35 probate or letters of administration, cancel the registration of the affidavit of the intestacy of the person whose will has been so proved, or to whose effects letters of administration with the will annexed have been so granted, and thenceforth the registration of the affidavit of intestacy shall have no operation or 40 effect whatsoever.

(8.) Proceedings shall not be taken as having terminated within
the meaning of this section until after the expiration of the time
allowed by law for appealing from the order granting or refusing
such probate or letters of administration, or if an appeal shall have
b been duly brought, until after the decision of the appeal.

20.—(1.) When probate of any will registered under this Act, or
letters of administration with such will annexed, has or have been
revoked by any court of competent jurisdiction, the registrar shall,
upon proof to him in the prescribed manner of such revocation
10 cancel the registration of the will, and thenceforth the registration
thereof shall have no operation or effect whatsoever.

(2.) Nothing in this section contained shall affect in any way
the priority herein-before given to any person claiming for valuable
consideration under any registered assurance executed by any
15 person claiming immediately or derivatively under any will registered under this Act where the assurance has been registered
prior to the cancelling of the registration of the will.

PART III.

JUDGMENTS AND JUDGMENT MORTGAGES.

30 *Judgments, Lis pendens, Crown Bonds, Recognizances, &c.*

21. After the commencement of this Act no judgment entered
up or made on or before the fifteenth day of July one thousand
eight hundred and fifty, nor any revival of any such judgment, nor any
recognizance, Crown bond, or lis pendens, shall affect any land
25 as to purchasers, mortgagees, or creditors, unless the same has
been duly registered or re-registered in the Registry of Judgments
or in the Registry Office within *five years* before the execution of
the assurance vesting or transferring the legal or equitable right to
the estate or interest in or to any such purchaser or mortgagee for
30 valuable consideration, or as to creditors within *five years* before
the right of such creditor accrued.

A.D. 1891.

Abolition of Registry of Judgments, and index of judgments to be kept.

22.—(1.) After the commencement of this Act the Registry of Judgments shall be abolished.

(2.) An index shall be kept in the prescribed manner and in the prescribed office of the High Court, for the registration of such judgments as may be prescribed.

(3.) The fees to be charged for indexing and searching in the index of judgments, and inspecting the judgments indexed, shall be deemed to be included in the fees mentioned in the eighty-fourth section of the Supreme Court of Judicature Act (Ireland), 1877; and the provisions of that Act relating to fees shall apply to such fees.

40 & 41 Vict. c. 57. s. 84.

Provision for registration of judgments, &c. in the Registry Office.

23. Any person who may require to register or re-register any judgment or revival entered up or made on or before the fifteenth day of July one thousand eight hundred and fifty, or any recognizance, Crown bond, or lis pendens may lodge in the Registry Office a memorial containing the prescribed description and particulars. Every such memorial shall have subscribed or attached thereto a certificate of the existence of the judgment, revival, recognizance, Crown bond, or lis pendens described therein signed by the proper officer in that behalf, or a certified copy of such judgment, revival, recognizance, or Crown bond, or of the material portions thereof, signed by such officer.

No judgment, lis pendens, recognizance, &c. to affect land other than that specified in the memorial.

24. The registration or re-registration of every such judgment, revival, recognizance, Crown bond, or lis pendens shall be effected in the prescribed manner, and no such judgment, recognizance, Crown bond, or lis pendens shall affect any land as to purchasers for valuable consideration, mortgagees, or creditors, other than the land specified in the memorial for the registration of the same.

Registrar to give certificates of registry.

25. The Registrar shall, whenever thereunto requested, after the lodgment of a memorial of any judgment, revival, recognizance, Crown bond, or lis pendens, or of any memorandum for the registry of satisfaction, vacate, or cancellation of the same, give a certificate in the prescribed form of such registry or re-registry, or of any registry or re-registry of any judgment, revival, recognizance, Crown bond, or lis pendens, or of any satisfaction, vacate, or cancellation contained in any book which shall, under the provisions of this Act, be transferred from the Registry of Judgments to the Registry Office, with a reference to the volume and page whereby the entry thereof may be readily found, and every such certificate shall be conclusive evidence of the registry or re-registry as therein stated.

26.—(1.) Any person desiring to register in the Registry Office a satisfaction, vacate, or cancellation of any judgment, revival, recognisance, Crown bond, or lis pendens, which has been registered in the Registry of Judgments and entered in any book which
5 shall be transferred to the Registry Office, or which shall be registered under the provisions of this Act, may lodge in the Registry Office a memorandum in the prescribed form referring to such judgment, revival, recognisance, Crown bond, or lis pendens, and having subscribed or annexed thereto a certificate of
10 the entry of satisfaction upon the roll of such judgment or revival; or in the case of a recognisance or Crown bond a certificate of the vacate or cancellation thereof, or an office copy of any quietus or certificate, or order in the nature of a quietus obtained by any debtor or accountant to the Crown, and of the certificate or
15 consent of the Attorney-General for Ireland; or in the case of a lis pendens, a certificate of the vacate thereof, such certificate to be signed by the proper officer in that behalf (and which certificate respectively such officer is hereby authorised and required to give), or a certified copy duly authenticated of such judgment, revival, or
20 recognisance, or of the material portions thereof respectively, and of the entry of satisfaction, vacate, or cancellation thereon.

(2.) The Registrar shall, upon the lodgment of any such memorandum for the registry of a satisfaction of any judgment or revival, or of the vacate or cancellation of any recognisance, Crown bond,
25 or lis pendens, cause a note of such satisfaction, vacate, or cancellation to be entered in the prescribed manner.

Judgment Mortgages.

27. No writ of elegit or writ of execution (save as hereinafter mentioned) shall issue or be sued against any land upon any
30 judgment entered up, or made after the fifteenth day of July one thousand eight hundred and fifty, nor shall any land be charged or affected by any such judgment, save as provided by this Act.

28. Where any legal or equitable estate or interest in or any disposing power over any land has, under any instrument
35 executed after the fifteenth day of July one thousand eight hundred and fifty become vested in any person as a purchaser for valuable consideration, such land shall not be taken in execution under any writ of elegit or writ of execution (save as hereinafter mentioned) to be sued upon any judgment entered
40 up or made before the fifteenth day of July one thousand eight hundred and fifty against such person, and no receiver shall be

[100.] D

A.D. 1901.

A.D. 1891.

appointed over such land in respect of any money due upon such judgment, nor shall such judgment operate as a charge upon or in anywise charge or affect such land, save as provided by this Act; but nothing herein contained shall take away or affect any rights or remedies which might have been had in relation to such land 5 if the Act of the session of the thirteenth and fourteenth years of the reign of Her present Majesty, chapter twenty-nine, had not been passed, in respect of any estate, interest, right, title, or power in, to, or over the same, which may have been in such person before the said day. 10

Creditors under judgments, &c. entered up or made after 15 July 1850, may file and register affidavit of ownership of land, and creditors under Judgments, before their debts may file and register a like affidavit in respect of land purchased after that date. (13 & 14 Vict. c. 29, s. 6.)

29.—(1.) Where (a) any judgment has been entered up or made after the fifteenth day of July, one thousand eight hundred and fifty, in a superior court at Dublin or in the High Court, or any decree, order, or rule to which the effect of a judgment in one of the superior courts of common law is given by an Act of the session 15 held in the third and fourth years of the reign of Her present Majesty, chapter one hundred and five, is made after the said day, or any judgment has been entered up or made in or by any inferior court of record after the said day, and has under the provisions of the last-mentioned Act been removed into a superior court at 20 Dublin or into the High Court, and the creditor under any such judgment, decree, order, or rule knows or believes that the person against whom the same is entered up or made is seized or possessed at law or in equity of any land, or has any disposing power over any land which he may without the assent of any other person 25 exercise for his own benefit; and where (b) any judgment has been entered up or made before the said day in a superior court at Dublin, or any decree, order, or rule to which the effect of a judgment in one of the superior courts of common law is given by an Act of the session held in the third and fourth years of the reign 30 of Her present Majesty, chapter one hundred and five, is made after the said day, or any judgment has been entered up or made in or by any inferior court of record before the said day, and has been under the provisions of the last-mentioned Act removed into a superior court at Dublin or into the High Court; 35 and the creditor under any such judgment, decree, order, or rule knows or believes that the person against whom the same is entered up or made is seized or possessed as aforesaid of, or has such disposing power as aforesaid over, any land which, by virtue of this Act, is exempted from being taken in execution under any writ of execu- 40 tion to be issued upon such judgment, decree, order, or rule, it shall be lawful for such creditor, at any time after the entering up,

making, or removal of such judgment, decree, order, or rule in, by,
or into such superior court or the High Court, or the passing of
this Act, whichever shall last happen, to make and file in the
High Court an affidavit (in this Act called an " affidavit of owner-
5 ship").

(2.) Every affidavit of ownership shall be in the prescribed form,
and shall state—

    (a) the name or title of the cause, action, or matter, and the
    court or division in which the judgment has been entered up
10   or made, and the date of the judgment;

    (b) the names, and the usual or last known place of abode, and
    the title, trade, or profession of the plaintiff (if there be such),
    and of the defendant or person whose estate is intended to be
    affected by the registration;

15   (c) the amount of the debt, damages, costs, or moneys recovered
    or ordered to be paid by the judgment:

    (d) that, to the best of the knowledge and belief of the deponent,
    the person against whom the judgment is entered up or
    made is at the time of the swearing of the affidavit so seised
20   or possessed, or has such disposing power as aforesaid, of or
    over such land;

    (e) the county and barony, or the city and parish, in which
    the land to which the affidavit relates is situate, and where
    such land lies in two or more counties or baronies, or parishes
25   or streets, or partly in one barony, parish, or street, and partly
    in another, the same shall be distinctly stated in the affidavit.

(3.) The creditor making the affidavit may register the same
by depositing an office copy thereof in the Registry Office; and
the affidavit shall be entered in the books and indexes kept therein
30 in like manner as if the same were a memorial of an assurance.
For the purpose of such entries the creditor under the judgment shall be deemed the grantee, the debtor thereunder shall
be deemed the grantor; the amount of the debt, damages, costs, or
moneys recovered or ordered to be paid thereby shall be deemed
35 the consideration; and the like fee shall be paid on such registration
as in the case of registering an assurance.

30.—(1.) Any number of persons jointly interested as creditors Affidavit may be made by certain persons, and are not
in relation to such judgment, and all joint stock banking and
other companies and corporate bodies shall be included in the term
40 creditor for the purposes of this Act.

A.D. 1891.

(2.) Every affidavit or oath necessary to be made by any creditor may be made by any one or more of such persons so jointly interested, by the public officer authorised to sue or be sued or to make oaths on behalf of such joint stock company, or by the secretary, deputy secretary, managing director, manager, or law 5 agent of any corporate body.

(3.) In any affidavit made by any such public officer, secretary, deputy secretary, managing director, manager, or law agent, a description of the town or place where the business or principal office of such joint stock company or corporate body is carried on or 10 situated shall be a sufficient description of the usual place of abode of the deponent, within the meaning of this Act.

(4.) Where any creditor is authorised to file an affidavit as aforesaid, and where, from the absence of such creditor or other reasonable cause, the affidavit cannot be made by him, it may be 15 made by such person as the court shall direct, and no registration of any judgment shall be invalid by reason of the affidavit being or having been made by one only of several creditors.

31.—(1.) The registration of an affidavit of ownership shall, subject to the provisions of this Act, transfer to and vest in the 20 creditor registering the same the land mentioned therein, for all the estate and interest of which the debtor mentioned in the affidavit shall at the time of registration be seised or possessed at law or in equity, or might at such time create by virtue of any disposing power which he might then without 25 the assent of any other person exercise for his own benefit, but subject to redemption on payment of the money owing on the judgment mentioned in the affidavit: and such creditor, and all persons claiming through or under him, shall, in respect of the land, or such estate or interest therein as aforesaid, have 30 all such rights, powers, and remedies whatsoever as if an effectual conveyance, assignment, appointment, or other assurance to such creditor of all such estate or interest, but subject to redemption as aforesaid, had been made, executed, and registered at the time of registering the affidavit. 35

(2.) Registration of an affidavit of ownership shall not operate as a waiver of any existing right or equity which the creditor may have against the land at the date of the registration.

(3.) Any creditor registering an affidavit of ownership may state therein that the affidavit is intended to be registered as against 40 some estate or interest therein particularly specified, less than the entire estate or interest of the debtor in the land, and where such

statement is made, the registration of the affidavit shall transfer   A D 1891
to and vest in the creditor the lands therein mentioned for such
lesser estate or interest only.

32. When an affidavit of ownership in respect of any judgment   Cancelling of
5 is registered, the registrar, upon the lodgment of a certificate   registration
of the satisfaction or performance of the judgment, signed by the   ownership to
proper officer in that behalf, shall cause a memorandum of satis-   operate as
faction, in the prescribed form, to be subscribed to the several   satisfac-
entries of the affidavit in the books of the registry office, and
10 shall also cancel the registration of the affidavit, and such registration shall thenceforth be deemed and taken as null and void : and
the legal or other estate in the lands affected by such registration
shall, without any further deed, conveyance, or assurance, be vested
in the person in whom such legal or other estate would have been
15 vested at the time of such cancelling if no such registration had
been effected.

33. Where an affidavit of ownership is registered, every such   Provisos
conveyance and other act whatsoever made or done after the   in 10 Chas.
date of the judgment mentioned in such affidavit, affecting any   I as to
20 land mentioned therein as would be deemed void against pur-   voluntary
chasers under an Act of the Parliament of Ireland passed in   up and as
the tenth year of King Charles the First, intituled an Act against   to fraudulent
covenous and fraudulent Conveyances, shall be void as against   conveyances.
the creditor registering such affidavit, and the like remedies may   [13 & 14 Vict.
25 be had in respect of such lands as if such conveyance or other   c. 29, s. 8.]
act had not been made or done; and nothing herein contained
shall in anywise affect the provisions of the same Act concerning
conveyances and other acts had or made to the intent to delay,
hinder, or defraud creditors.

30 34. All such chattel interests in lands as might have been taken   Act not to
in execution under any writ of fieri facias if the Act of the session   affect exe-
of the third and fourth years of the reign of Her present Majesty,   fieri facias.
chapter one hundred and five, had not been passed, may be taken   [3 & 4 Vict.
in execution and otherwise dealt with under any writ of fieri facias   c. 29, s. 10.]
35 already issued or hereafter to be issued, notwithstanding anything
in this Act contained.

35. In the administration in any court of the assets of any person   Rights of
against whom any judgment has been or shall be entered up   judgment
or made either before or after the commencement of this Act, who   administra-
40 shall die seised of or entitled to any land, the creditor under such   tion of assets
judgment shall have the same rights upon and in respect of such   preserved
land as if this Act had not been passed.   [13 & 14 Vict.
c. 29, s. 11.]

A.D. 1891.

Priority of
judgment
mortgages
for poor
rates.
[12 & 13 Vict.
c 104. s. 18.]

36. Every civil bill decree for poor rates filed in the High
Court under the provisions of the seventeenth section of the Act of
the session of the twelfth and thirteenth years of the reign of Her
present Majesty, chapter one hundred and four, may be registered
as a judgment mortgage against any land situated within the union 5
where such poor rates have accrued due, of which at the time
of swearing the affidavit of ownership for the registration of the
same the person against whom such civil bill decree has been
obtained, is seised or possessed at law or in equity, or over which
at the said time he has any disposing power which he may without 10
the assent of any other person exercise for his own benefit. Every
such civil bill decree registered as a judgment mortgage, and every
judgment for poor rates registered as a judgment mortgage, shall
take priority as a charge on all the estate and interest in any land
of the debtor mentioned in the affidavit of ownership, and situated 15
in the poor law union wherein the poor rates for which such civil
bill decree or judgment was obtained accrued due, before all charges
and incumbrances whatsoever, except Crown rent, quit rent, tithe

5 & 6 Vict.
c. 89.

rentcharge, charges existing under the Act of the session of the fifth
and sixth years of the reign of Her present Majesty, chapter 20
eighty-nine, and the Acts amending the same, and charges existing

10 & 11 Vict.
c. 32.

under the Act of the session of the tenth and eleventh years of the
reign of Her present Majesty, chapter thirty-two, and the Acts
amending the same.

PART IV.   25

HOW REGISTRATION SHALL BE EFFECTED.

Ordnance Map to be the basis of Registry.

Registration to
be effected
against the
denominations
upon ordnance
map.
[13 & 14 Vict.
c 72 s 1.]

37. The ordnance map shall form the basis of registration
under this Act, and of the indexes and books to be kept thereunder, and (except as hereinafter expressly provided) every 30
assurance, disposition, or instrument registered under this Act shall
be registered only against the denominations on the ordnance
map.

Registration to be by Memorial.

Registration
effected by
delivery of
memorial.

38.—(1.) Registration shall (except where the contrary is ex- 35
pressly provided) be effected by the delivery to the registrar of a
memorial in the prescribed form of the assurance, disposition, or
instrument proposed to be registered.

A.D. 1891.

(2.) The person delivering such memorial shall deliver with it a certificate in the prescribed form, stating the number of folios contained in the memorial, the number of grantors and of denominations, and stating (except in the case of provisional registration) that the denominations in the memorial are denominations on the ordnance map, and stating such other matters as may be prescribed.

(3.) Every memorial shall be authenticated in such manner as may be prescribed.

(4.) It shall be the duty of the registrar at the prescribed time, and in the prescribed manner, to ascertain that each memorial complies with the requirements of this Act; and in the case of an assurance or will (if such assurance or will shall be produced to the registrar) to compare the memorial with the assurance or will.

(5.) The rules under this Act may provide for the comparison of the memorial prior to registration in certain particulars only, and for a subsequent comparison (if necessary) in order that the memorial may constitute a sufficient foundation for the books and indexes to be kept in the office, and on any such comparison the memorial may be amended by the registrar in any respect in which it is found to be erroneous.

39.—(1.) The person delivering the memorial of an assurance or will may at the same time deliver to the registrar a copy of the assurance or will at full length, subject to the prescribed conditions; and it shall be the duty of the registrar to compare such copy with the assurance or will, if the same shall be produced to him, and, if it is a true copy of the assurance or will, to endorse upon the copy a certificate to that effect, in the prescribed form.

(2.) A copy of such assurance or will, certified by the registrar to be identical with the copy so lodged, shall be delivered to any person requiring the same on payment of the prescribed fee, and such last-mentioned certificate shall be conclusive evidence that the copy so certified is a true copy of the assurance or will.

40. Every memorial (other than a memorial for the purpose of provisional registration) and every affidavit of intestacy shall specify the denominations on the ordnance map, and the county and barony in which each denomination is situated, or (in the case of land situated in a city) the city and parish in which each denomination is situated, and in addition shall contain the several statements which may be prescribed in respect of every assurance, disposition, or instrument registered under this Act.

Provisional Registration in certain Cases.

41. Where an assurance, disposition, or instrument contains no description of any part of the land comprised therein or affected thereby, or where the name of any land described in such assurance or disposition shall not correspond with the denominations on the ordnance map, and it shall be desired to register such assurance, disposition, or instrument provisionally, in order to preserve its priority, and until a perfect registration can be effected, the person seeking to register the same may deliver to the registrar a memorial thereof in the prescribed form; whereupon, and upon all the other requirements of this Act having been complied with, the registrar shall enter such assurance, disposition, or instrument in the prescribed manner as provisionally registered, and shall give to the person registering the same a certificate to that effect.

42. An affidavit of ownership may be admitted to provisional registration as of course upon the certificate of the person seeking to register the same, or his solicitor, that such affidavit does not correctly state the denominations on the ordnance map of the land sought to be affected. If within the prescribed time there is delivered to the registrar a memorandum in the prescribed form stating the denominations on the ordnance map, then the registration of such affidavit of ownership shall become absolute and effectual, to all intents and purposes, as of the date of such provisional registration, and the registrar shall cancel the entry of such registration as provisional, and enter such registration in the books and indexes of the registry office as of the date of such provisional registration; but if such memorandum shall not be so delivered as aforesaid within the prescribed time, then such provisional registration shall be null and void, and of no effect whatever.

43. If within the prescribed time from the provisional registration of any assurance, disposition, or instrument a perfect memorial thereof shall be delivered to the registrar in the prescribed form, the registration of such assurance, disposition, or instrument shall become absolute and effectual, to all intents and purposes, as of the date of the provisional registration, and the registrar shall cancel the entry of such registration as provisional, and enter such registration in the books and indexes of the registry office as of the date of the provisional registration, and shall give a certificate of registration in the prescribed form; but if a perfect memorial is not so delivered as aforesaid within the prescribed time, then the provisional registration shall be null and void, and of no effect whatever.

44. The registrar shall not admit any assurance, disposition, or instrument (other than an affidavit of ownership) to provisional registration unless upon the production to him of an affidavit made by the person seeking to register the same, or his solicitor, stating
5 that immediate registration is required, and that the person seeking to register the same is unable to state the names of the denominations on the ordnance map.

45. While any assurance, disposition, or instrument remains provisionally registered the same assurance, disposition, or instrument
10 may be registered in the ordinary manner by any person authorised to register the same, and in the event of the provisional registration becoming absolute, the subsequent registration of the same assurance, disposition, or instrument shall be cancelled by the registrar, otherwise the same shall be as valid and effectual as if the assurance,
15 disposition, or instrument had not been so provisionally registered as aforesaid.

Proof of Execution of Instrument Registered.

46.—(1.) Any assurance, the execution whereof by the grantors appears to be attested by two witnesses (at the least), whose names
20 and addresses are thereto subscribed or therein stated, may be registered within one year from the date at which it purports to have been executed, without proof of execution, upon production of the assurance to the registrar; and for this purpose the date at which an assurance purports to have been executed means, in the case of
25 an assurance purporting to have been executed by more than one grantor at different times, the earliest date at which it purports to have been executed by any grantor.

(2.) When any assurance does not appear to be so attested, or has been executed more than a year previously, or is not produced
30 to the registrar, its execution shall be proved in the prescribed manner.

47.—(1.) Any will, in respect of which probate, or letters of administration with the will annexed, has or have been granted by any court of competent jurisdiction, shall be admitted to registration at
35 any time without proof of execution, upon production to the registrar of such probate or letters of administration, as the case may be, or a copy stamped with the seal of the court.

(2.) Any will to which there is an attestation clause, by the terms of which it appears that the will was duly executed in accordance
40 with the provisions of the Acts for the time being regulating the execution of wills, may be registered within *two years* from the

A.D. 1891.

death of the testator, without proof of execution, upon production
to the registrar of such will and on proof in the prescribed manner
of the death of the testator.

(3.) When any will has not such an attestation clause as herein-
before is mentioned, or has been executed more than two years 5
previously, its execution shall be proved in the prescribed manner.

Assurances or Wills more than Thirty Years Old.

Assurances or wills more than thirty years old may be registered under order of the Court.

48. When any assurance or will proposed to be registered is
more than thirty years old, and its execution cannot be proved
as hereinbefore provided, the person seeking to register the same 10
may apply to the High Court, in the prescribed manner, for an
order directing such assurance or will to be registered, and the
High Court, if satisfied that such assurance or will comes from
the proper custody, and that its execution cannot be proved as
hereinbefore provided, may order that the same shall be registered ; 15
and the registrar, upon production to him of such order, shall
register such assurance or will without requiring proof of its
execution.

Registration of Lost Assurances or Wills.

Memorial of lost assurances or wills may be registered under order of the Court.

49. If any assurance or will has been lost, the person seeking 20
to register the same may apply to the High Court in the prescribed
manner, for an order directing that a memorial of such assurance
or will be received and registered ; and the Court, if satisfied that
such assurance or will has been lost, and if the contents and
execution of such assurance or will are proved to its satisfaction, 25
may order that a memorial of such assurance or will be received
and registered, and the registrar, upon production to him of such
order, shall register such memorial without requiring proof of the
execution of the assurance or will.

Production of Assurance to Registrar. 30

Except in certain cases the assurance or will shall be produced to the registrar.

50. Every assurance or will shall be produced to the registrar
along with the memorial, except—

(1.) Where the assurance or will, has been lost ;

(2.) Where a court of competent jurisdiction has granted probate
of such will or letters of administration with such will annexed, 35
as the case may be ; or

(3.) Where the assurance has been executed out of Ireland by
any grantor, or the will has been executed out of Ireland,
and it is not sought to have such assurance or will, registered

under the provisions herein-before contained without proof of A.D. 1891.
execution.

Certificate as to Memorial.

51. Any person registering any assurance, disposition, or
instrument, other than a lost assurance or will, shall certify in
writing that the contents of the memorial are correct, and if
he shall wilfully sign a false certificate he shall be guilty of a
misdemeanor.

Proceedings when the Registrar shall refuse to accept Memorial.

52.—(1.) When any memorial delivered to the registrar for the
purpose of registration under this Act does not comply with the
requirements of this Act, or is not in the prescribed form, or
contains statements other than those herein-before provided or prescribed, the registrar may refuse to receive such memorial, and
shall, if requested by the person tendering any memorial so rejected
by him, deliver to such person a statement in writing of his reasons
for his refusal to receive the same.

(2.) The registrar shall, if requested by the person tendering such
memorial, register conditionally the assurance, disposition, or
instrument in the prescribed manner, and shall give to the person
tendering the same for registration a certificate to that effect.

53.—(1.) The person tendering such memorial may, if he be
dissatisfied with the rejection of the same by the registrar, apply
to the High Court, in the prescribed manner, within the prescribed
time, for an order that such memorial be received by the registrar,
within a time to be named in the order, and the court, if of opinion
that such memorial ought to have been received by the registrar,
may make an order to that effect.

(2.) On production to the registrar of such order of the High
Court within the time named therein, he shall receive such memorial,
and shall proceed with the registration of the assurance or disposition
of which it is a memorial, and such registration shall be effectual to
all intents and purposes as of the date of such conditional registration,
but if such order is not made, or not produced within such time,
the provisional registration shall be null and void and of no effect
whatever.

Power to compel Registration in certain cases.

54.—(1.) Any person claiming any interest in land under any
assurance or will which has not been registered, may in writing

require any person in possession of the original document, or (where the original document is lost) a copy of or extract from the original document, to deliver or send the same at or to the registry office, for the purpose of its being registered, or to produce the same before a judge of the High Court for the purpose of having 5 an order made in relation to the registration of the same; and in case the person in whose possession the same shall be refuse so to do, the judge, upon application in the prescribed manner, may make such order respecting the delivery or sending of such document or copy or extract as aforesaid, at or to the registry office, or the 10 production thereof before him for the purpose aforesaid, as he shall think proper.

(2.) Nothing in this Act contained shall authorise any person to require or enforce the registration of any assurance, or will, or copy, or extract, in case any agreement or provision for the non- 15 registration of such assurance or will shall have been made by him or by any person from or through whom he derives an interest under such assurance or will.

(3.) The costs of such application and of the registration of the assurance or will shall be in the discretion of the judge, and he 20 may order that an attested copy of the original document, or of the copy or extract to be delivered or sent as aforesaid, shall be furnished to the party by whom the same shall be so delivered or sent at the expense of the party by whom the application is made.   25

55. Provision may be made by general rules for the registration in the prescribed manner of any disposition other than those by this Act directed to be registered, and such rules may in the case of any such disposition prescribe as to the persons who shall be deemed to be grantors and grantees respectively in relation thereto, 30 and as to the entries to be made in respect of such registration.

PART V.

GENERAL PROVISIONS.

Certificate of Registration.

56. The registrar upon the delivery to him of a memorial in the 35 prescribed form, and upon proof of the execution of the assurance, will, or disposition proposed to be registered in the cases in which such proof is required, and upon all the other requirements of this Act having been complied with in the prescribed manner, shall

register the assurance, will, or disposition, a memorial of which has A.D. 1891.
been so delivered to him, in the books of the registry office in the
prescribed manner. He shall also indorse a certificate of registration in the prescribed form on every assurance, disposition, or
5 instrument produced to him, and when the assurance, disposition,
or instrument registered has not been produced to him, shall give to
the person registering the same a certificate in the prescribed form.

57. Every such certificate shall be conclusive evidence that the *Certificate to
be conclusive*
assurance, disposition, or instrument has been duly registered at the
10 time in the certificate stated, and a certificate of provisional or conditional registration shall be conclusive evidence that the assurance,
disposition, or instrument therein mentioned has been provisionally
or conditionally registered at the time in the certificate stated.

Registration only effectual against Lands mentioned in Memorial.

15   58. No assurance, disposition, or instrument shall be considered *Registration
effected by
memorial of
a memorial.*
as registered against any land other than the land mentioned
in the memorial for the registration of the same; but the
registration of any assurance, disposition, or instrument as to
certain of the land comprised in or affected thereby shall not
20 prevent its subsequent registration as to any other land comprised
therein or affected thereby.

Provisions as to Notice, &c.

59. All priorities given by this Act shall have full effect in all *Priorities to be
enforced, and-
notwithstanding
notice, except
in case of
actual fraud
[1 & 2 Vict.
c. 11. s. 23.]*
courts, except in cases of actual fraud, and no person shall lose any
25 priority under this Act merely in consequence of his having been
affected with notice, actual or constructive; but, notwithstanding
anything herein contained, it shall be lawful for a court of competent jurisdiction to deprive any person of the priority to which
he would otherwise have been entitled, on the ground of actual
30 fraud.

60. Nothing in this Act contained shall to confer on any person *Priority of
persons claim-
ing for valuable
consideration.*
claiming without valuable consideration under any person any
further priority or protection than would belong to the person
under whom he claims.

35   61. The registration of any assurance or disposition which if *Void assurance, &c.
validated by
registration.*
unregistered would have been fraudulent and void, shall not prevent
such assurance or disposition from being fraudulent and void in
like manner as if the same had not been registered.

A.D. 1891.

Registration of Caveats.

Person to enter
a caveat.
[13 & 14 Vict.
c. 72. s. 42.]
62.—(1.) Any person may, by a requisition in writing under his hand in the prescribed form, require a caveat in respect of any land mentioned in such requisition to be entered on behalf of any person therein described. 5

(2.) When such requisition is delivered by any person other than a solicitor, it shall be accompanied by an affidavit in the prescribed form stating the interest of the person by whom it is delivered and the land mentioned in such requisition.

(3.) Every caveat shall be in the prescribed form, and shall state— 10
1. The date on which it is delivered.
2. The name and addition of the person by whom it is delivered.
3. The name and addition of the person on behalf of whom it is delivered.
4. The time for which it is intended to remain in force, which 15 shall not exceed *six months.*
5. The denominations on the ordnance map of the land intended to be affected by such caveat.

Mode of entering caveats.
[13 & 14 Vict.
c. 72. s. 43.]
(4.) When a caveat is so required to be entered an entry shall be made in the prescribed manner, and containing the same parti- 20 culars as if it were an assurance affecting the land mentioned in such caveat, and executed by the person requiring such caveat to be entered.

Extent of protection to be afforded by caveat.
[13 & 14 Vict.
c. 72. s. 13.]
63. When a caveat is entered as to any land, every person claiming for valuable consideration under any assurance affecting the 25 same land executed by the person by whom the entry of the caveat has been required, or any person claiming under him, to or with the concurrence of the person on behalf of whom the caveat was so entered, or his heirs, executors, administrators, or assigns, and registered within the period mentioned in the caveat after the caveat 30 shall have been so entered as to such land, shall be entitled to the same priority, under this Act as if such assurance had been executed and registered at the time of entering the caveat.

The protection of caveats restricted to specified cases.
[13 & 14 Vict.
c. 72. s. 14.]
64. No caveat shall be of any force or effect, except by way of protection to a contract entered into at or before the date of the entry of 35 the caveat, or by way of protection to an assurance for valuable consideration made or executed in pursuance of such contract, or by way of protection to any assurance for valuable consideration which at the date of the entry of the caveat shall have been executed by some one or more of the persons by whom the land shall be 40 conveyed or otherwise affected, or by way of protection to an

A.D. 1891.

assurance for valuable consideration which was in contemplation at the date of such entry; and no caveat shall have any force or effect as against the operation of the bankruptcy of the person requiring any caveat to be entered, or any act under such bankruptcy.

PART VI.

SEARCHES.

65. All persons interested in making searches may search and examine the indexes and books kept in the registry office, and may take abstracts or other short notes of any of the matters in such books, and also inspect, in the presence of some person belonging to the said office, any original memorial or assurance upon paying the prescribed fee for such search and inspection respectively.

Common Search.

66. Upon a request in writing being left in the registry office, a common search shall be made, and a copy of the abstract of every memorial, and of every memorial within the terms of the request, shall be made, and signed in the prescribed manner, and the same shall be delivered to the party making the request; and the person making such request may except thereout any assurance or disposition.

Search and Negative Certificate.

67.—(1.) Every person requiring a search and negative certificate to be made shall lodge with the registrar a requisition in the prescribed form.

(2.) The person making such requisition may limit or extend the search and certificate in such manner as may be prescribed with reference either to names of persons, denominations, exceptions, period of time, or generally as to any other such matters as may be prescribed.

(3.) The registrar shall, upon the delivery of the requisition, cause a search to be made and give to the person making such requisition a certificate in the prescribed form and containing abstracts or copies, as may be prescribed, of all memorials within the terms of the registration.

A. D. 1891.

Searches for Judgments.

Requisition for searches for judgments, &c. in the registry office.

68. Any person requiring after the commencement of this Act a search to be made in the registry office for judgments, revivals, recognizances, Crown bonds, and lis pendens, or any of them, and a certificate of such search, may lodge with the registrar a requisition 5 in the prescribed form. The registrar shall upon the lodgment of such requisition cause a search to be made, and give to the person delivering such requisition a certificate in the prescribed form.

Duplicates.

Requisition for duplicate searches in registry office.

69.—(1.) Any person requiring after the commencement of this 10 Act a duplicate of any search or certificate, or a copy of any search recorded under the statutes in force before the commencement of this Act, may lodge with the registrar a requisition in the prescribed form, and the registrar shall, upon the lodgment of such requisition, cause such duplicate or copy to be made and given to the person 15 requiring the same, with a certificate stating that the same is a duplicate of the search and certificate in such requisition mentioned or a copy of the recorded search, as the case may be.

(2.) Every such duplicate or copy so certified as aforesaid shall have the same force and effect, and shall be accepted and required 20 in the same manner and for the same purposes as an original certificate or recorded search to the same extent and in the same forms.

Requisitions.

Requisition by solicitor. (7 & 1 W. 4, c. 37. s. 77.)

70. Any person may lodge a requisition by his solicitor; but 25 in that case it must be expressly stated in the requisition that the solicitor lodging the same is solicitor for the person on behalf of whom the requisition is lodged.

PART VII.

CONSTITUTION OF THE OFFICE.—STAMPS AND FEES.   30

Keeping registry office to be carried on under the Act.

71.—(1.) From and after the commencement of this Act the registry office established by the Act of the sixth year of the reign of Queen Anne, chapter two, shall be carried on under the provisions of this Act, and all books and documents at any time used or kept in the said registry office shall be public property, and be preserved as herein-after mentioned.

(2.) There shall be kept in the registry office such indexes and books as shall be prescribed.

72.—(1.) The establishment of the registry office shall consist of a registrar, and such officers and clerks, *with such salaries or remuneration as the Land Judge, with the approval of the Treasury, shall think fit, to be paid out of moneys to be provided by Parliament.*

(2.) Nothing herein contained shall affect the tenure of office or salaries or remuneration of the existing registrar or either of the existing assistant registrars.

(3.) On and after the first vacancy in the office of registrar after the commencement of this Act, the following provisions shall take effect with respect to that office. Any person appointed to be registrar shall be a person then serving in the office of not less than *ten years* service, or a practising barrister or solicitor of not less than *ten years* standing, or a person who has served as registrar of judgments for not less than *ten years*; he shall be appointed by the Land Judge, and he or any officer or clerk in the office may be removed for inefficiency or misconduct.

(4.) The registrar, before entering upon office, shall give security for the due performance of the duties of his office in such manner and to such amount as the Land Judge, with the approval of the Treasury, may direct.

(5.) All persons appointed after the commencement of this Act to be officers or clerks in the registry office, with the exception of the registrar, shall be appointed by open competition, and the Lord Chancellor shall, with the concurrence of the Civil Service Commissioners, make regulations as to the qualification of candidates and the subjects of examination, and all officers and clerks in the registry office shall hold their offices by the tenure of ordinary civil servants of the Crown.

73. The registrar and all other persons employed in the registry office shall execute their respective offices in person, and not by deputy, unless where a deputy for the registrar or any such person shall be appointed for that purpose by the Land Judge in the case of temporary illness or other sufficient cause of absence; and no officer of the registry office shall, during the term of his

A.D. 1891.

holding office, directly or indirectly practise as a barrister or solicitor, or participate in the fees of any other person so practising.

Office to be under the management of the registrar.
[5 & 3 W. 4. c. 67. s. 4.]

74. The management and superintendence of all departments in the office shall devolve upon the registrar; but in order to facilitate the business of the registry office (but nevertheless without in any way diminishing the responsibility of the registrar for any act or omission) the assistant registrars and any officer hereafter appointed to discharge duties analogous to those of the existing assistant registrars may, for and on behalf of the registrar, take affidavits, sign official documents, and do all official acts necessary in the execution of the duties of the registry office.

Stamps and Fees.

Fees payable to the office.
[5 & 3 W. 4. c. 87. s. 5.]

75. The Treasury, with the concurrence of the Land Judge may by order fix, and may alter or vary the fees to be taken in the registry office, in respect of memorials, searches, certificates, affidavits, or other acts, instruments, or matters relating to registration, to the intent that the same shall be justly apportioned, and that no greater fees shall be charged than will amount to a sum sufficient to discharge the expenses of the registry office. The fees taken at the time of the commencement of this Act shall continue to be taken until an order is made under this section, and thereafter in so far as they are not varied by such order. The Public Offices Fees Act, 1879, shall apply to the Registry Office, and to the fees appointed to be taken therein.

42 & 43 Vict. c. 58.

No document to be received or used unless stamped.
[97 & 48 Vict. c. 14. s. 6.]

76. If at any time it shall appear that any document has through mistake or inadvertence been received, or filed, or used without having the proper stamp impressed thereon or affixed thereto, it shall be lawful for a judge of the High Court, if he thinks fit, to order that such stamp shall be impressed thereon or affixed thereto, and thereupon when a stamp shall have been impressed on such document or affixed thereto in compliance with any such order, the document and every proceeding in reference thereto shall be as valid and effectual as if the stamp had been impressed thereon or affixed thereto in the first instance.

PART VIII.

A.D. 1891.

GENERAL RULES, AND MISCELLANEOUS PROVISIONS.

78. The Land Judge, with the approval of the Lord Chancellor, may, by order, make general rules for carrying into effect the objects of this Act, and in particular without limiting the foregoing power in respect of all or any of the following matters; that is to say,

(*a.*) The regulation and management of the registry office;

(*b.*) The indexes and books to be kept in the office;

(*c.*) The mode of entering therein the registration of assurances, dispositions, and instruments by this Act authorised to be registered;

(*d.*) The mode of entering therein and numbering caveats;

(*e.*) The searches to be made and certificates to be given, so far as they are not provided for by this Act;

(*f.*) The forms of memorials, of affidavits, of requisitions for searches, of certificates of searches, and of certificates of registration of assurances, dispositions, and instruments, and also such other forms or directions as he may deem requisite or expedient for carrying out the provisions of this Act; and

(*g.*) The several matters in this Act mentioned as to be prescribed.

General rules to be framed after passing of Act.

79. The authority for the time being having power to make rules of court for the purposes of the Supreme Court of Judicature Act (Ireland), 1877, may, in the manner prescribed by the sixty-first section of the same Act, make rules of court as to all or any of the following matters, that is to say :

Rules for the keeping of the Index. 40 & 41 Vict. c. 57.

1. The office of the High Court wherein the Index of Judgments is to be kept.

2. The manner in which such index is to be constructed and kept.

3. The judgments which are to be indexed.

4. The method which is to be followed for supplying information for the construction and keeping of the index; and

5. The transfer of books, indexes, and other documents from the Registry of Judgments to the Registry of Deeds, or to such public office or offices as they shall direct; and they may determine the time at which every such transfer shall be carried out.

A.D. 1891.

Provision as to adoption of printing &c. improvements.

79.—(1.) The Land Judge, with the consent of the Treasury, may direct that printing or any scientific improvement shall be introduced and made use of in the registry office, and may make such provisions as they may think fit for the purpose of having the efficiency of any mechanical invention or other improvements 5 tested, by the adoption of the same for a limited period, or for certain defined purposes, and may direct the adoption of any mechanical or other inventions or improvements in relation to the making and keeping of the indexes and books in the registry office, or in relation to the making of searches therein. 10

(2.) So soon as printing or other improvements shall be introduced into the registry office in lieu of scriveners, it shall be lawful for the Land Judge, with the approval of the Lord Chancellor (notwithstanding anything herein contained to the contrary), by general rules, to substitute for a memorial of any assurance, will, 15 affidavit of intestacy, or disposition a full copy or counterpart thereof, and to direct in what manner such copy or counterpart shall be made, and how it shall be authenticated for registration, and generally to make such further and other rules for the management and regulation of the registry office, and the mode of con- 20 ducting the business thereof, as the introduction of printing or any scientific improvements shall render necessary or expedient.

Extension of Time.

Extension of time may be granted for good cause.

80. In any case in which this Act provides, or in which any rule to be made as herein-before is mentioned shall provide, that any 25 matter or thing may only be done within a fixed time, the Court may, for good cause, extend the time fixed by this Act, or such rule, as the case may be, on application made in the prescribed manner either before or after the expiration of that time.

Affidavits. 30

Persons before whom affidavits for purposes of Act may be sworn.

81. Affidavits for any purpose under this Act may be sworn before the registrar or such other officer as may be prescribed (each of whom is hereby empowered and required to administer oaths); or before a judge of assize; or before any justice of the peace; or before a person authorised by law to take affidavits in 35 causes and matters depending in the High Court.

Treasury may defray expenses of completing indexes, &c.
[? & W. &
L. J. & M.]

82. It shall be lawful for the Treasury, from time to time, out of such moneys as may be provided by Parliament for that purpose, to defray the expenses of compiling, transcribing on parchment, and completing any memorials, transcripts, or indexes, remaining 40

A.D. 1891.

incomplete in the registry office, and of printing the same, or any
part or parts thereof, and also of preparing the books directed
by this Act to be prepared, and also of introducing printing or
scientific improvements into the registry office, and also of the
5 adoption of such inventions or improvements as are herein-before
mentioned, or of testing the efficiency of the same; and it shall
be lawful for the Treasury to make such provisions as they may
think proper for having copies of the Ordnance maps and indexes
kept under the control of the clerks of the various unions through-
10 out Ireland, or other public officers, for the use of the public, in
order to facilitate registration under this Act.

83. In all proceedings before any court for all purposes whatsoever an office copy of any memorial shall, upon such copy being
proved in like manner as an office copy of any other record, be
15 received and taken as evidence of the contents of the memorial
of which it purports to be an office copy without the production of
the original memorial.

84. If any person shall forge or counterfeit, or cause or procure
to be forged or counterfeited, or knowingly act or assist in forging
20 or counterfeiting the name, signature, or handwriting of any officer
of the registry office, in any case in which the signature of such
officer is or shall be required or authorised to be made; or shall
forge or counterfeit, or cause or procure to be forged or counterfeited, or knowingly act or assist in forging or counterfeiting the
25 name, signature, or handwriting of any person whomsoever to any
document which is or shall be required or directed to be signed by
such person; or shall, with an intention to defraud any person
whomsoever, use any document, the signature to which shall be so
forged or counterfeited as aforesaid, knowing the same to be forged
30 or counterfeited; or shall sign his own name, or cause or procure the
signature of the name of any other person to any certificate or
other writing requiring to be signed by an officer of the registry
office; or shall use any such certificate or other writing with the
intent to defraud thereby any person whomsoever, any such person
35 so offending, being thereof lawfully convicted, shall be and is hereby
declared guilty of felony, and being convicted thereof shall be liable,
at the discretion of the court, to be imprisoned for any term not
exceeding *two years*, with or without hard labour.

Registrar of Judgments.

40 85. The Registrar of Judgments, and the clerks in the Registry
of Judgments, shall, notwithstanding the abolition of that office, be

A.D. 1891.

10 & 41 Vict.
c. 57.

attached to the Supreme Court of Judicature, and shall be subject to
all the provisions relating to officers contained in the Supreme Court
of Judicature Act (Ireland), 1877, as amended by any other Act,
and the paragraph of the seventy-second section of the Supreme
Court of Judicature Act (Ireland), 1877, as amended by any other 5
Act, which relates to the power to transfer an officer from a
Division in which his services are not required to some other office
of the High Court or some Division thereof, shall apply to the
Registrar of Judgments and to the clerk in the Registry of
Judgments as though they were officers attached to a Division; with 10
this addition in the case of the clerk, that he may be transferred by
the Lord Chancellor, with the concurrence of the Land Judge,
to the Registry, and may be required to perform such duties in that
office as the Land Judge may appoint. If in the case of either of
the said officers a transfer is not effected within the prescribed time 15
the officer not transferred shall be released from office and shall be
entitled to such compensation as the Treasury shall consider reasonable and proper, having regard to his tenure of office, and to all the
other circumstances of the case.

Repeals and Savings. 20

Repeal of
former Acts
with saving
clauses.

86.—(1.) The Acts in the schedule to this Act described are
hereby repealed to the extent appearing in the third column of the
schedule.

(2.) Every assurance or disposition registered under any of the
Acts repealed by this Act shall have the same priority as the same 25
would have had if such Acts respectively had not been repealed.

(3.) Subject to the provisions of this Act relating to the registration and re-registration in the registry office of the judgments
and other dispositions heretofore requiring registration or re-registration in the registry of judgments, and subject also to the pro- 30
visions of this Act relating to the registration of wills where the
testator shall die after the commencement of this Act, nothing
contained in this Act shall be construed as requiring the registration
of any assurance disposition or instrument executed or made before
the commencement of this Act, when under the law as it previously 35
existed such assurance disposition or instrument would not have
required registration in the Registry of Deeds.

Effect of
registration
under this Act
of assurances
required to be
registered

87.—(1.) Where the registration in the Registry of Deeds of any
assurance disposition or instrument is provided for by any Act in
force at the commencement of this Act, such assurance disposition 40
or instrument may be registered under this Act (subject to the

provisions of the same), and the provisions of any such Act with
regard to the registration of any such assurance or disposition
shall be satisfied by the registration of the same under this Act.

(2.) This section shall apply to the duplicate of an order with
5 respect to the making of a loan made by the Commissioners of
Public Works in Ireland and required to be registered in the
Registry of Deeds under the provisions of the Act of the session of
the tenth and eleventh years of Her present Majesty, chapter
thirty-two.

10 88. In this Act, unless there is something in the context in-
consistent therewith,—

"Addition" means description as to residence, title, rank, pro-
fession, condition, or occupation.

"Assurance" means any deed, conveyance, or writing (other
15 than a will), whereby any estate or interest in, or charge
upon land is created, appointed, conveyed, assigned, extinguished, evidenced, or affected, at law or in equity, and unless
where the contrary is expressly provided, includes an assurance
executed or made before or after the commencement of this
20 Act, and includes such writings as are in this Act declared to
be assurances.

"City" includes town, borough, county of a town, county of a
city, and county of a town and city.

"Crown bond" includes judgment at the suit of the Crown,
25 statute, inquisition, and acceptance of office.

"Denominations" means names of divisions of land to be
affected by registration within a county or city, as the case
may be, and "denominations on the ordnance map" means
the names of such divisions as the same appear on such map.

30 "Devisee" means any person taking any estate or interest in
land under a will, including an administrator with the will
annexed, and includes any person claiming through or under
an immediate devisee.

"Disposition" means any act, affidavit of ownership, or matter
35 affecting land, and any dealing with land, other than an
"assurance," as herein-before defined, or "will," and unless
where the contrary is expressly provided includes a disposition
made before or after the commencement of this Act.

"Equitable mortgage" means any charge created by deposit
40 of title deeds without an assurance, and includes solicitor's
lien.

"Execution" includes signature. In the case of assurances not
under seal.

A.D. 1891.

Act of Parliament.

10 & 11 Vict. c. 32.

Interpretation clause.

"Grantee" means any party to or person claiming under an
assurance other than a grantor, and includes any person
claiming through or under an immediate grantee.

"Grantor" includes any party to an assurance by whom or under
them of such assurance any estate, interest, or charge in or upon   5
land, is created, appointed, conveyed, extinguished, evidenced,
or affected; and in the case of a disposition affecting land,
shall mean every person whose estate or interest in such land
is affected by the disposition.

"Judgment" includes order and rule of any superior court,   10
decree and order in any court of equity, order in bankruptcy
and lunacy, and judgment, order, decree, and rule of any
inferior court.

"Judgment mortgage" means an affidavit of ownership registered under the provisions of the Act of the session of the   15
thirteenth and fourteenth years of the reign of Her present
Majesty, chapter twenty-nine, and any Act amending the
same, or under the provisions of this Act.

"Land" includes lands, messuages, tenements, or hereditaments of
any tenure, held for any estate, legal or equitable, and whether   20
corporeal or incorporeal, and any undivided share thereof, and
any estate or interest therein; and also any charge upon, or
issuing out of lands, tenements, or hereditaments, whether
such charge be or be not secured by a term of years, or by any
other estate in lands, tenements, or hereditaments.   25

"Lease" includes an agreement for a lease.

"Lord Chancellor" includes Lord Commissioners and Lord Keeper
of the Great Seal of Ireland.

"Order affecting land" means any judgment, decree, or order
of a court of competent jurisdiction by which any estate or   30
interest in land is or may be created, declared, transferred, fore-
closed, charged, determined, or otherwise affected.

"Ordnance map" means the ordnance survey map made and
published under the direction of the Commissioners of Works
in Ireland.   35

"Prescribed" means prescribed by any general rules made, or
forms or directions issued, in pursuance of this Act.

"Registered" means duly registered in pursuance of the provisions of this Act.

"Registrar" and "general rules" mean such "registrar"   40
and "general rules" as are in this Act respectively in that

before mentioned, and " registrar " includes assistant registrar A.D. 1891
or deputy registrar.

" Registry office " means the office for registering assurances,
wills, affidavits of intestacy, and dispositions under this Act.

" Registry of Judgments " means the office established by the 7 & 8 Vict.
Act of the session of the seventh and eighth years of the reign c. 90.
of Her present Majesty, chapter ninety.

" Will " includes a codicil and any testamentary document
executing a power of appointment.

SCHEDULE to which the foregoing Act refers.

[Note.—Those enactments which have been already repealed are included in this schedule, to avoid the necessity of reference to previous statutes.]

Date of Act	Title of Act	Extent of Repeal.
6 Anne, c. 2. (I.)	An Act for the public registering of all deeds, conveyances, and wills that shall be made of any honours, manors, lands, tenements, or hereditaments.	The whole Act.
8 Anne, c. 10. (I.)	An Act for amending an Act intituled An Act for the public registering of all deeds, conveyances, and wills that shall be made of any honours, manors, lands, tenements, or hereditaments.	The whole Act.
6 Geo. I. c. 14 (I.)	An Act for explaining and amending two several Acts in relation to the public registering of all deeds, conveyances, and wills.	The whole Act.
25 Geo. III. c. 47. (I.)	An Act for amending the several laws relating to the registering of wills and deeds in the registry office of this Kingdom, and for the better regulating and conducting the business of the said office.	The whole Act.
3 Geo. IV. c. 116.	An Act for the more convenient and effectual registering in Ireland deeds executed in Great Britain.	The whole Act.
4 Geo. IV. c. 57.	An Act to provide for the regulation of the public office for registering memorials of deeds, conveyances, and wills in Ireland.	The whole Act.

Date of Act	Title of Act	Extent of Repeal
10 Geo. IV. c. 50.	" An Act to consolidate " and amend the laws " relating to the man- " agement and improve- " ment of His Majesty's " woods, forests, parks, " and chaces, of the land " revenue of the Crown " within the survey of " the Exchequer in Eng- " land; and of the land " revenue of the Crown " in Ireland; and for " extending certain pro- " visions relating to the " same to the Isles of " Man and Alderney."	Section 62.
6 & 7 Wm. IV. c. 87.	An Act to regulate the office for registering deeds, conveyances, and wills in Ireland.	The whole Act.
7 & 8 Vict. c. 90.	An Act for the protection of purchasers against judgments, Crown debts, lis pendens, and cognovits of bankruptcy, and for providing an office for the registering of all judgments in Ireland; and for amending the laws in Ireland respecting bankrupts and the Evaluation of actions.	Sections 2, 3, 6, 9, 10, and 11; the proviso at the end of section 17; section 21, section 22, so far as relates to the appointment and duty of the Registrar of Judgments, section 40.
11 & 12 Vict. c. 120.	An Act to facilitate the transfer of landed property in Ireland.	The first nine sections and the schedule.
12 & 13 Vict. c. 104.	An Act to amend the Acts for the more effectual relief of the destitute poor in Ireland.	Section 16.
13 & 14 Vict. c. 29.	An Act to amend the laws concerning judgments in Ireland.	The whole Act except section 12.
13 & 14 Vict. c. 72.	An Act to amend the laws for the registration of assurances of lands in Ireland.	The whole Act.

Date of Act	Title of Act.	Extent of Repeal.
18 & 14 Vict. c. 74.	An Act for the better regulation of the office of Registrar of Judgments in Ireland.	The whole Act. 5
20 & 21 Vict. c. 60.	The Irish Bankrupt and Insolvent Act, 1857.	Section XIII, the part to the words following, "and required according to the provisions of the Act of the seventh and eighth years of the reign of Her present Majesty, chapter 90." Section XId. 10
22 & 23 Vict. c. 105.	An Act to amend an Act of the thirteenth and fourteenth years of Her present Majesty, to amend the laws concerning Judgments in Ireland.	The whole Act, except section 2. 15
27 & 28 Vict. c. 76.	An Act to make valid defective registrations of deeds in certain cases, and to substitute stamps in lieu of the fees now payable on proceedings in the Registrar of Deeds Office in Ireland.	The whole Act, except sections 1 and 2. 20 25
34 & 35 Vict. c. 72.	An Act for the further protection of purchasers against Crown Debts, and for amending the laws relating to the office of the Registrar of Judgments and other offices of the Court of Chancery, Ireland.	The whole Act, except sections 1, 73, and 84, and Schedule 4. Schedules B and C. 30 35
38 & 39 Vict. c. 3.	An Act to amend the law relating to the Registry of Deeds Office, Ireland.	The whole Act.
46 & 47 Vict. c. 20.	The Registry of Deeds Office (Ireland) Holidays Act, 1883.	The whole Act. 40

Registration of Assurances (Ireland).

A

BILL

To consolidate and amend the Laws relating to the Registration of Deeds and Judgments, and to provide for the Registration of other assurances, acts, and matters affecting Land in Ireland.

(Prepared and brought in by Mr. Attorney General and Mr. Arthur Balfour.)

Ordered, by The House of Commons, to be Printed, 5 February 1891.

PRINTED BY EYRE AND SPOTTISWOODE,
PRINTERS TO THE QUEEN'S MOST EXCELLENT MAJESTY

And to be purchased, either directly or through any Bookseller, from
EYRE and SPOTTISWOODE, East Harding Street, Fleet Street, E.C.; and
32, Abingdon Street, Westminster, S.W.; or
JOHN MENZIES & Co., 12 Hanover Street, Edinburgh, and
90 and 91, West Nile Street, Glasgow; or
HODGES, FIGGIS, & Co., 104, Grafton Street, Dublin.

[Price ½d.]

[Bill 190.]